Picture Word
PRAYERS

A of prayers for little

Mary E. Erickson

Illustrated by Jane Conteh-Morgan

STANDARD PUBLISHING

God's Love

Dear heavenly Father,

The  tells me, "God is love."

Your love is higher than the and .

It's deeper than the .

It's stronger than the mighty ,

and it reaches all around our .

You love every  and , every and , and all the .

You made us a wonderful to live in, with in the and in the , with in the and in the .

I know you love me, God. I love you too.

For a New Day

Good morning, God!

Your warm  is shining through my .

A perched in a is chirping a happy song.

My friendly jumps on my and licks my .

The and the and my make me smile.

Thank you, God, for this new day.

Mealtime Prayer

Dear God,

Thank you for the  and  on our  .

Thank you for  and  and  .

Thank you for  and  and  .

Thank you for filling our  with good things to eat.

My Wonderful Body

Dear God, you made my body special!

Thanks for my [hands] that pet my [cat],

and for my [feet] that jump high in new [shoes].

Thanks for my [nose] that smells [cookies] baking,

and for my [mouth] that eats those [cookies] and [pizza] too!

Thanks for my  that see and

and for my that hear flying in the .

Thanks for my that can throw a and give a .

You gave me a wonderful body, God.

God's Animals

God, you made every animal special.

You gave the  a long neck

so he can reach the on the tops of tall .

You gave the a powerful tail

to help him swim in the and leap high for .

You gave the polar thick white fur

to keep him warm in the land of and .

You gave the  a special

so she can carry her wherever she goes.

You gave my a curly tail

that she can wag to say she likes me.

Thank you, God, for making each animal special.

Christmas

Thank you, God, for Christmas.

I like to hear what the  says about the first Christmas,

when Jesus came to our

and slept in a .

I like to hear about  who guarded their

and  who filled the night  and sang good news.

I like to hear about the  who traveled on

and followed a to bring  to Christ the king.

Thank you, God, for  Jesus and for Christmas.

Four Seasons

Thank you for the seasons, dear God.

I like spring, when  bloom

and the wind blows my high in the sky.

I like summer, when the is hot and we

swim in the or run through the .

I like autumn, when honking  fly south

and we jump in piles of crunchy .

And I like winter, when sticks to the

and we slide on a down a slippery .

Thank you, God, for the fun and beauty of each season.

School Prayer

Dear God, thank you for my school.

I'm learning lots of exciting things.

I know that a 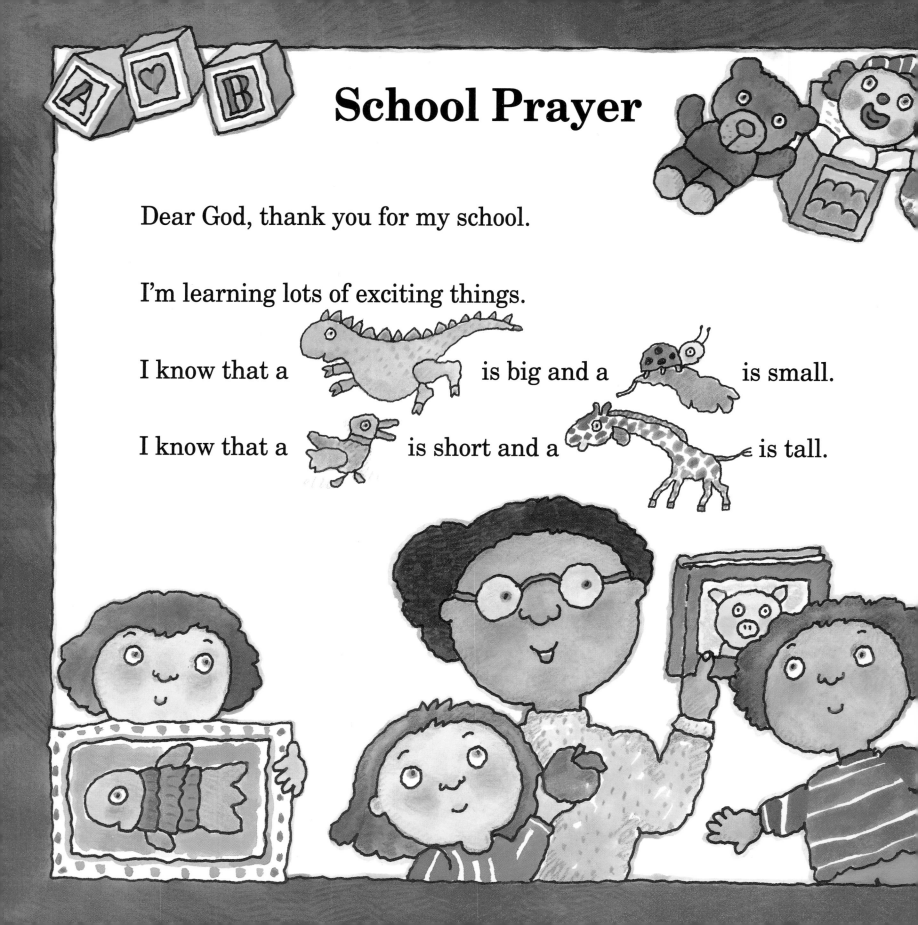 is big and a is small.

I know that a is short and a is tall.

I can paint with a  and listen to my read a

about a on a farm or a in a brook.

I'm learning to share with and

when we play on the or with and .

Bless my and my friends, dear God.

For People Who Help Us

Thank you for  who help us, God.

For the who puts out a ,

and for the who keeps our safe.

Thank you for the and the

who help me when I'm ,

and for the  who grows the I eat.

Thank you for the and

who protect our country in and on .

Thank you for all these helpers, God. Keep them safe and well.

Bath Time

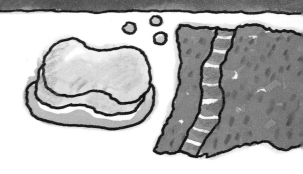

Dear Jesus, I like bath time.

Thank you for the  I splash in the .

Thank you for my  and  that float

and for my  sponge and slippery 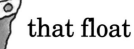.

Thank you for my fluffy 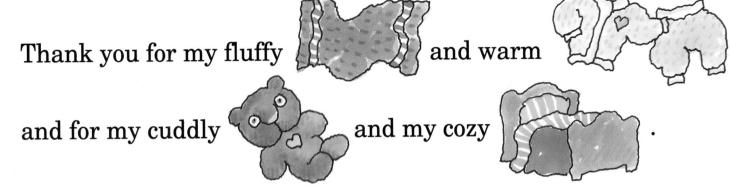 and warm

and for my cuddly and my cozy .

Thank you for being my friend. Good night, dear Jesus.